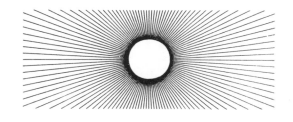

Pottersfield Press

Rainbow Warehouse

by

Ann Knight and W.P. Kinsella

Pottersfield Press
Lawrencetown Beach, Nova Scotia
Canada

Published with the support of The Canada Council
and the Nova Scotia Department of Tourism and Culture

Canadian Cataloguing in Publication Data

Knight, Ann.

  Rainbow warehouse.

  Poems.
  ISBN 0-919001-55-6

I. Kinsella, W.P.   II. Title

PS8571.N54R35 1989   C811'.54   C89-098589-8

Cover artwork by Lee Harwood
   (with suggestions by Harvey Chometsky)

Authors' photograph by Brian Kent

Published by:
Pottersfield Press
Lawrencetown Beach
RR 2, Porters Lake
Nova Scotia BOJ 2SO
Canada

Contents

RAINBOW WAREHOUSE

A Mantra
For Regaining a Grasp On The Present

AK

now
now
now
not now or now
or now

a moment's notice
a moment's peace
a moment later

then
back then
when we decided to live just now -
and I knew I could do it forever
and you knew you could do it for now

the same bargain I have going with you -
        I have going with death
        I have going with hope
        I have going with fear
        I have going with giving
        I have going with taking
        I have going with loving

I have going with just making it through

        and in, and always now
        now, and yet anew,
        now

the mystery of grasping the present, constantly
moving hand over hand

to keep from sliding into the past
to keep from losing the hold by gazing
too far ahead on the rope
      now
      hand over, now
      over hand,
      now, hand over hand
      now
      over

Rainbow Warehouse

WPK

Where do rainbows go?
Is there, somewhere
a warehouse full of rainbows
disassembled
piled in neat bundles,
greens here, blues there,
waiting?

Like rainbows
the street girls
appear and disappear
gaudy, interchangeable
where do they go?
Where are last year's whores?

Perhaps, somewhere, there is
a warehouse
full of rainbow women
disassembled
piled in neat bundles
arms here, torsos there,
waiting.

Magic Man

your wife raises rabbits
attends to the habits of doves
when you come home, your children
search your pockets, discover
scarves or glasses full of water
at no time is the mystery of your calling
discussed with reverence among them -
they align trinkets to measure
the circumference of your fame

regulate your breathing
make our nickels disappear
there's more to staging miracles
than we're prepared to hear
undulate into and out of
whatever fetters you choose ·
the water-filled torture chamber
a dead mentor passed along? yes,
we'll gladly see you in it under tons of sand

there is more to sleight-of-hand
than your vow of silence can explain

For Poets Only

As we entered
your apartment
an image dropped
on me.
It will probably
make me famous,
if I don't forget it.

May I write it
on your arm?
It's not a tattoo
for God's sake!
I just want my mind clear
for loving you.
If you'd undo
just one more button
I could inscribe it
on your breast.
Red pen is painless,
warm as lipstick.
It is not kinky! Okay,
then let's go to bed.
But I warn you,

my mind
will be elsewhere
until I scratch
that image
into your shoulders
or bite it into
your thighs.

morning thoughts of a former lover

AK

laying breakfast oranges out -

ouch! . . .the knife we used

to cut everything in sight

Recalling Tomorrow

AK

In their silent joydance they wake me
sometimes, the lightshades crossing behind
my eyelids or before my open eyes.

And if I ask their meaning,
they send a member forward to paint
a glowing answer in the air: a name
I recognize, a gesture I recall.

This uncertain space is fragrant
where their knowing collects my sorrow
and recollects an approaching 'morrow -
so I may find reason to sing.

As dawn erases these delicate
lights, my midnight dancers,
I am amnesiac again.

Holy Mary

though her feet are bare
the long underwear tells
it is winter
as she dances before the
hot water heater
slicing the vegetables
that will become
tonight's stew

there are so few
who remember the rituals
of a holy war
and anymore, she is
our town's last anomoly,
the one we entertain
the hungry tourists with -
those who will pay
the price of one girl's freedom

flower-child sister, now
fallen-woman mother,
we try to sing-a-long, but
we cannot see
what steps to take
to imitate your dance,
and yes, we know, we love our boots
more highly than we ought

4 a.m.

WPK

Curbed taxis doze
outside a late cafe.
Boys on a bus bench
slump, hands on knees,
as sulky-faced girls
smoke and beg quarters.
First names and empty pockets.
Streets blue before dawn.

Winter Lake

WPK

From a squinting sky
tines of fierce sunlight
pierce
the pitch-fork morning.

I Am Joaquin

WPK

In the sage-brush distance
Joaquin Murieta
rides at full gallop
toward the mission
of San Luis Obispo,
a black sombrero
shielding his Aztec eyes,
a Mexican baby in each saddlebag.

Scars

WPK

Behind the house,
roses,
patches of satin
among the rubbish
where fat brown bottles
lounge like rats
as wind thrashes the willows
that tick like claws.
A storm rolls in.

Thunder shivers the house,
lightning fries branches against the sky.
We children watch
as rain strafes the windows,
flattens the grasses,
makes the window glass cool.

Afterward,
in the rainsweet yard
we collect petals,
damp them to our faces
where they dry like scars.

November 22, 1963
AK

Thursday, after our choir practiced for Sunday night's
concert, I told Cathy, "The Brahms Requiem is
beautiful, but no one has died."

My father snatched his camera, kissed us both and
    took off on foot
to cross the few blocks to the elevator. Sirens made
    my heart pound.
Soot rained. A tense odor pressed in. My nostrils
    would not resist,
nor could my throat. The tighter night drew herself
    down dark upon us,
the more vibrant the fiery show flashing on the
    cyclorama above.
An entire harvest -my mother repeated- an entire
    harvest, lost.
It's beautiful, my father announced when he returned
to pack a lunch and drink water from his hands held
    under
the tap. They can only control the periphery. She's
    going to come down.
Even the grain catches fire as it pours out the blazing
    walls. The Night
the Elevator Burned Down etched the hot spectrum of
    disaster on my life.

Friday night, our debate colleague, Carl, grabbed
several cameras - left for Dallas, in a borrowed car.
At the hospital on Sunday he shot
one photo: Lee Harvey Oswald, delivered by screaming
ambulance with wounds as mortal as the President's.
And I had reason to sing.

21

The American Dream, II

WPK with Mildred Kinsella

Kitchen faced woman,
You slice antiseptic vegetables
Calm eyes circling the room,
Riding like grapes
On a stainless steel knife,
Head divided in cannisters,
The left eye salt, the right sugar,
Flour-bin forehead perpetually wrinkled
As you think of new ways to disguise hamburger.

A metallic sink is your hidden lake,
Frying pan barges sink in prophylactic hands,
Dry busy fingers on porcelain apron,
While a water drop rolls like an agate
Across the mirrored floor,
Robot children with vanilla blood
Clank by, mouths and brains
Stuffed with chocolate chips.

Bedside

WPK

His arms are wax white
like the peonies my mother
has placed beside his bed.
His hands
in the empty air above his head
twist and glide
splicing cable as they did
a half century ago.
He plaits the strands
like a woman tending her child's hair.

The mine and the town
where he learned his trade
have been abandoned, the cable
rusted back to earth
only the skill remains
a permanent tenant
in his pale fingers.

His eyes open,
faded as dried flowers
they stare
straight past his hands
and he looks so calm,
his mind, perhaps
splicing strands of time
back to when he had a young wife
and an armful of daughters
waiting for him after work.

Methods

WPK

To avoid them
>I peer around corners
>with periscope eyes,
>walk close to buildings
>melt into doorways
>when cars screech to a halt.

To confuse them
>I hang garlic wreaths
>on their doorknobs
>while they are out
>searching for me.
>They occupy a building
>where one might meet
>white mice in the corridors
>or discover carrots
>hidden in latrines.

To escape them
>I have moved three times:
>my address is now a peach tree
>at the foot of a mountain.

Sparrows at the Drive-In

WPK

Across a cold chainlink fence
a honeysuckle bough intrudes,
its berries,
bright as fresh-drawn
beads of blood,
ignored by birds
who, scruffy as winos,
waddle and hop on hoods
in a fawning dance.

Bloated, dull-eyed addicts
stuffed with grease
cadge crumbs of fatty fries
and pasty bread,
beg foolishly to be
filled with more emptiness.

Across the lot
in the honeysuckle bush
no birds flit or chirp
tart orbs wither
amidst green glitter
as luscious berry flesh
goes uneaten.

Oedipus Poem

WPK

Poem, on the road to Thebes
meets an old man
quarrels over the right-of-way
strikes him with a staff
watches as eyes roll white
as old fingers talon the dust.
Poem, striding toward destiny
prepares to answer questions
frail ankles full of fire

*The Will

(a found poem)   AK

If I ever be gone to Paradise:
trapline for my grandson,
the house for the boys, and
some stuff for D. S. who can
take care of Tina 'til she is of age
to look after herself

I want every thing
in perfect order just as if
me and Zeke was alive

S. K. is the boss for this house and
he will be responsible for everything

***Signed and witnessed on an Indian reserve
in British Columbia, 1974.**

27

Natural Barriers

I've been throwing my voice again.

I slide my hand into the words, sending these fingers
upwards into your language as far as they will go.
Although we pretend to have met before,
it's always the first time. The life I signal
sets a seal on our limbs, "Strong as death."

We can never be seduced from what we do best.

I can hold you whether it is mountains
or raging rivers you would cross.

"How is this done? We can hear the poet singing
a river into place, but we haven't seen her lips move."

I told you. What I'm doing
is done at the tips of my fingers.

Ignore the tongue. Like water, it's a natural barrier.

ROADSONGS

vignettes from a 1982 book promotion tour AK

1.   Wait for us. We are migrants
        harvesting a cash-and-carry crop
        of audacious impressions from your fields -
        keeping between us the taut counterpoint
        of luscious metaphor and magic question.
        Doesn't imagination always dance with drifters?

2.   And should we toss these maps
        aside and drive at will, pulled
        by the slant of summer's longer light
        or the sounds of stretching corn? No.
        Agreed on paths and passages chart
        our way of moving into dawn.

3.   What I like about making love
        on the road, is the taming
        of so much territory -claiming parts
        of the continent for ourselves alone,
        putting weary bone and flesh down
        where others may not have tried.

4.   What I like about making love
at home, is being closer to
the floor, knowing where the door
is, and how the interruptions flow.
I can invent stories there, and
bring the unfamiliar in, to play.

5.   No one mentioned we'd be competing
with other "artists" at Arts Day.
Literature didn't hold its own against
free balloon rides, condoms, and hypnotists.
Someone sat up nights devising this:
"Two Poets vs. Trained Police Dogs."

6.   We could make room for him -
that hitchhiker we've seen twice today.
But would he want to hear
Kroetsch read? Does he care for
words, or What The Crow Said?
I might give him a wave.

7. If I could caress a song
    bringing up every shade of sadness,
    I'd sing of former journeys, lonesome
    ones, undertaken without you for company.
    Hearing the pain, I'd be grateful
    our paths never crossed, but collided.

8. I was busy counting the celebrities
    we'd met at George Anthony's party,
    when you cut in to observe,
    "It was good we went once.
    Now we know we aren't missing
    anything if we never go again."

9. "Look at this, papa," Hazel says.
    "Tulips for us -all the way
    from Calgary," although she can see
    from the card, I bought them
    in town. Homecooked dinner, talk, sunset.
    We string a narrative beyond midnight.

10.   Salinger took Kinsella as a pseudonym -
wrote <u>Shoeless Joe</u> himself to test
today's literary climate from a distance,
gossips in the Big Apple assert.
"Mr. Salinger is outraged and offended. . .,"
his lawyers write on snowy stationery.

11.   Union City, New Jersey, has re-elected
Bill Musto its mayor -despite his
recent criminal conviction on charges mandating
seven years behind bars. But, why?
"I love these Union City people,"
Musto weeps, "and they love Musto."

12.   People don't recognize themselves as characters.
You've told me that. But I'm
not a believer. I could disguise
loved ones; but certain tyrants speak
their misguided speeches unaided. Who could
ever hope to improve on them?

13.   I get a little nervous when
the clouds take a notion to
converse with me while you're napping.
Bunching across the horizon, they announce,
"Until people can empty the sky,
they'll continue to deny. . .God's within."

14.   Chir. Chir. . .wikka. Chir. . .wikka. . .chir.
Nebraska floats her evening critters forward -
fireflies flit above ditches, play peekaboo
in the cornfields. Mosquitoes and grasshoppers
(thick as flies) smash against the
windshield. We'll bed down early tonight.

15.   Similarities? No. Difference is what marks.
What all this moving and shaking
is like unto, can be imagined.
What I propose to deliver is
the-body-yet-to-be-imagined -
at the tips of our fingers.

16.   Imagine me on that ferris wheel,
a simple treadmill plowing the sky
with shrieks from the newly initiated.
You stay as you were, grounded
on a secure crust of earth,
the unchanging horizon in full view.

17.   You notice a woman intently digesting
the fine print I pasted on
the panels of our stalwart Datsun -
promotional copy for <u>Shoeless Joe</u>. She
looks up. "Sounds good. Have you
read it?" Too late, she realizes.

18.   At times, when my pace begins
to control me, instead of me
controlling my pace, I pause
to assess my breathing, and sing
the slower, sadder songs I know,
songs that draw out suffering's vernacular.

Postcard to Oleta

AK

It is enough that distance cannot remove our caring.

Pain is spoken in many languages. We divide

Mania and Depression - previously joined by the hip.

Our suffering is reflected in many places:

   Brown prairie grass struggles into spring because
   She has no one to assist with emptying the sky.

Hearing Confession

AK

for miles as we rode together
she spoke of his anxiety (with work)
and then she shifted to her own
(ineffectual efforts to change the routines
their lives had come down to) - in the kitchen,
in the games room, in the bathroom and,
of course, in the bedroom
finally, she confessed:
things seemed to work better when she
was totally in charge (in the kitchen, in the games room...)
but, she could feel
the truth welling up -
she did not want to be in charge in the bedroom
there, she wanted that boy who'd toyed
with her at sixteen, to transport her
to the backseat of that ancient Chevrolet once again
to throw his carelessness and hers against their bones,
pounding escapist excitement through their flesh
until they cried out exhaustion

all her efforts to get him to take responsibility for the bills,
for pouring the new sidewalk the city required, for doing
part of the housework, had been requests that he take charge
in the one room where she'd never wanted to give orders
she didn't know if it was too late
she knew she'd been afraid to speak about it
but speaking was cleansing her of a lie

she was ready to probe a mystery

VOWS

AK

the fluid I am, awash upon the
solid you are; that solid
now melting, now
joining -
eyes pulling eyes
and memory creeps upward and
over us; we lose all recollection of over

a fluid butterfly awash upon a
solid sunset; what's solid
is dissolving now, is
melting -
eyes let go of eyes
and memories wash up and
over me; I'm transparent again, color over

Longing

WPK

How I wish I might walk
in the kind of soft rain
that never washes
the perfume of the past away.

Why I Laugh

WPK

I sit on your sofa
trying to make
polite conversation,
failing,
because the only thing
on my mind
is touching you.
Just inside the door
my boots
yellow and scruffy
as tomcats
sit next to your
lithe, sequined heels.
The silences grow longer,
the tea colder,
I should either
make a pass
or go home.
I hear a scuffling
from the hallway
and picture
our shoes
fucking.

You wonder
why I laugh
and walk
toward you.

Friday, Like Your Laugh

AK

Friday, like your laugh, will be warm.
I'll pick a cadence of nerves off your body,
break open my flesh on your song.

> Like nomads surviving a heatwave
> we'll be found chanting at sunrise
> dancing towards life
> in the deserted canyons of the city
> singing of the skeletons and their secrets
> of the living and their charms.

Friday, like your laugh, will be sudden.
I'll cradle your days in the belly of my guitar.
Like troubadors, we'll move along with the sun.

Brambles For Ann

WPK

When I think of you
thin blue-clad skaters
speed through my veins
leaving long crimson trails.
See what you've done to me!

A locomotive chugs
through my hollow limbs

wheels pumping
like a sprinter's elbows,
All because I know
I'll see you in an hour.

You can pluck nerves
off my body
like sharp metal brambles.
Watch your fingers, love!

Woman, I want to drink
your blood! Blot your passion
with my body, twirl my tongue
in the honey of your thighs.
I'm beginning to care only of what
you think of me, and
the brambles bounce
like marbles on marble
as I throw them away.

For Ann

WPK

Tip back your head
smile
into my mouth
with your electric
tongue.

Tip back your head
as I tongue
the tips
of your nipples
hard,
trace warm trails
down your belly,
taste
the moistness. . .

Tip back your head
smile
into my mouth,
pass the pulsing
taste of love
the sweet sugar
of each other.

Highrise Thursday

AK

thunderperfect

you cross my horizon
lugging ten thousand opening lines
backlit by shimmering sundogs
(in the wings, as many future lovers
as I was still planning to take)

thunderperfect

we don't seem meant for each other
I could never settle down
into a highrise Thursday
(we don't speak or even sing alike,
yet we persist toward this duet):

thunderperfect

lounging beneath the highnoon trees -
we don't think to make a photograph,
memory will bring us here another time
(you were drinking while I ate, or
is it that I've stretched the song?)

Rosemary -1940

WPK

Rosemary, my almost sister
Kicked my hand
From Mama's belly
Before Mama went away
So full of joy
Returned with empty
Arms and eyes
(The baby
In a cardboard box
Unloaded like luggage
From the bowels
Of a Trailways bus.)

Oslin the Estonian
Mute from birth
Carpentered the casket
From birch
As lovingly as he
Carved the cradle
The lamb of God
Bleating head and foot.

In the funeral drizzle
My father's friends
Usually so jovial
Stood like stones
Their huge red hands
Poking from unfamiliar sleeves
Trying to comprehend.
Such helpless men
Able to fix anything
With baling wire
Except their children.

Mean Beginnings

When the water pipes freeze

 we bathe in winter light -shafts of it

 stream through the gunnysack curtains

 forming puddles on the floor.

Clothes off or on, we cleanse

 ourselves in the other's glance,

 mark this morning's passing

 by tracking the day's advance:

Now, an apparent flood staining the far wall.

 Snowstorms, dust, rain, or windstorms -

 We capitulate the Alberta seasons

 to invent: the eye of a lovestorm.

Vows
for Glen & Mamie, my grandparents   WPK

land
he chose
she lived on

food
he bought
she prepared

children he fathered
she nurtured; clothes
they needed, she fashioned

the hard of him -
an ambition to raise cotton where no one had
she held next to the hard of herself
the soft of him -
an abandon to loving and laughter
she pulled close to the soft of herself

at ninety
he continued, but she stopped
going to church on Sundays
doing the wash on Mondays

her frailty worried him;
the long-ago bargain to live and die together
without interference from catheters, oxygen,
transfusions -was his to keep
for the light in her eyes
was only occasional now

she was ready to go, and
he mustn't leave without her

One Generation
for Shannon   WPK

It's almost over
and my eyes fill with tears
as I look at her sleeping
half-child, half-woman.

Her doll lies loose
in the bend of her arm.
She smiles, dreaming of what
I'll never know,
for we grow farther apart
every day.

The curtain
with ballerinas
in pink and blue,
the dresser covered
with stuffed toys,
looking a little sad
as they are moved
farther back
to make way
for hairspray
and cosmetics.

Pictures of angels and kittens
are gone; long-haired musicians
stare at me from the walls
names I don't know
styles I don't understand
I will try to accept, but
one can only live
in one generation
at a time.

Letter Home

Full of words

in the middle

of the night: a letter home.

But by day

I censor them.

Unable to tell
how I felt after
Uncle Alfred
told me
to dance for him
stripped down
(age eight)
in the barn,
I cannot at eighteen
report: doing fine,
quite nicely
thanks, okay.

Across a decade one dance

taunts and lingers. The ghost

of my mother's brother

will not yet let me compose

a simple letter home.

EAST HASTINGS

a sequence based on observations in Vancouver, B.C.

BL 817.6 AR14D4

WPK

In the library
in a book by Diane Arbus
I see myself on every page.

She collected raw pain

could see beyond the skin

her subjects like peeled grapes

hung out their bloody

laundry for her wicked eye.

I see myself; each freak is me

bloated, beaten black,

murdered, eyes popped, slime

on my cheeks.

Behind the camera her eyes, razors

cut out a tumor

held it up

like a game ball.

Suicide was such
a soft release
from her agonized eyes.

BROKEN DOLLS

WPK

I am part birdsong
and part clay. Whimsical coffee.
Madness Tea. Brash, cynical, vulgar on paper.

I view life from the river's edge -
watch the flow, pick out morsels
that interest me: a cat
dainty-dipping in the fish bowl.

But it's hard to be brash
when you cry over broken dolls.
If my larksong cloak were peeled away,
baring my motives
pink and wiggling as newborn mice,
those who know such things
would say, I have spent most of my life
trying to repair
broken dolls.

WPK

World under water, under tears,
Porcelain ambulance slides down the curb,
Wine-splotch flasher flip-flops like sickness,
Fireworks scattered on windows and windshields,
Muscatel bottles far back in an alley,
Glint green like the pirate eyes of a cat,

Those who drink neon walk only at night,
Martian street lights watch, mute.
Sadie Rosebush, so far from the meadow,
Skirt askew, leans on an aluminum pine,
Spirits weep, as angels die drowned.
Silence is outcast,
Streets whimper and cry as pleasure pain
Rises on a car horn barometer,
Hum-whine of traffic, perpetual motion,
Slow eyes up from concrete
Bloodied in the siren's wail.
Shriek music from dark doorways,
Shrill voices like breaking glass,
Ears branded by the snickering click of pool balls,
The scraping walk of old feet,
The air-rifle snap of high heels on hard tiles.

Crystal brittle,
Diamond hard,
Edges gash,
Fingers tear,
Gentleness is dead,
Everything is the color of money
Words like stones from each sling-shot mouth,
Beery exhaust fans, the breath of the street
Spew cigarette smoke,
Neon Christ on a power-pole cross
Tambourine voices call a drunken dance on the concrete.

VET

WPK

A one legged man
leans on a parking meter
begs
spare change for a vet,
his face oily, unshaven.
He snarls at those who refuse,
mumbles of Dieppe,
curses the world
as he swats at a dog
with his crutch.

VOYEUR

WPK

Often I stand and watch while people sleep
Absorbing life that chatters in the air
The sweet odors of identity run deep
And feed my starving soul a substance rare.

BEER PARLOUR

WPK

Young black men
in felt fedoras
catfoot around
the pool table
while their blond
gun-eyed women
sight the bar.

PARANOIA

WPK

At the next table
they are talking about me,
heads together,
small, slug-like phrases
oozing down their teeth.

CUSTOM CUE

WPK

Like a doctor
he unsnaps his black case
revealing cold pearl,
smooth varnish,
slim, sensuous:
balanced solidity
nestled in a velvet pool.

Cue braced against thigh
an extension of himself,
he screws the stalk together,
gently, fondly.

In bright geometry
the balls gleam a challenge.
With clean, clipped strokes
he clears the table,
coolly collects bills.

His lady sits silent,
sips, smokes,
docile as a tame hen,
her small dull eyes
filled with longing.

SATURDAY NIGHT

WPK

Mink-eyed whores
with tattooed arms
patrol the sidewalk,
booted, bra-less,
cold as bullets,
they parade past hotels
full of creaking rooms.

OLD MEN

WPK

I have an abiding fear
of old men
who sit in hotel lobbies
brittle and dry as insects
mounted under glass;
old men who walk with canes
tap-tapping,
or cadge quarters
in beer parlour doorways
unshaven and shaking
with breath like lye;
I fear old men
sitting in bleak cafes
who stare into coffee, wondering
to whom they must apologize
for living so long.

AT THE MISSION

WPK

The cold room
grows thick
with brown breath,
bad feet, and
second-hand whiskey.
Shaking like wet dogs,
broke-backed men
let sermons land
between them
like soft grapefruit.

PARTY

Tazzie played with a dead rat.
Little bugger. Geez it was funny.

Annie's flat watermelon face suspended in ice,
Exhaust pipe mouth spraying beer-heavy
Smoke laugh at the stained ceiling. My eyes
Are drawn like magnets to the strange
Man-creature prints in the linoleum doorway
Offering a berserk opener-broken "smile."

Through the sad brown varnish of the bedroom door
I see Tazzie, brown as the door,
Shadow eyes drawn to the lightbulb.
No one else sees him, unobtrusive
His grey tee shirt pulled down,
Out of habit, to nearly his knees.
Where is my rat, he whimpers. Only I hear.

You know how to fix a camera?
It is thrust at me anyway. Broken
Polaroid covered with Tazzie's hands.
Overexposed pictures, rat-eye red,
All that is left of yesterday. Annie
With a beer and a smoke, smiling her pumpkin smile,
Beside her, Cliff grins from his tunnel mouth.

Them was before the fight,
Hell they had to be, I wasn't grinning after.
Always remember the good times,
The times before the fight, before the rat,
Before the skeleton chair upended in the corner,
Before the glass, before the blood,
Before the jam and vomit on the floor.
We never took no pictures of Tazzie.

Cory smiles a hazy smile, blowing smoke,
Holds out her hand to me.
Katie One-eye sleeps in a corner, while
Verlin-she-met-in-the-bar, lolls senseless
In a plastic chair, on the nod.
You got good veins -Cory's sepia hand
Like a shadow across my arm -easy to hit.

How could I know he'd die?
Maudlin tears, and beer
In the burning stomach of day,
Three hours to daylight, slow-motion time,
Sodden tempers swim-warm beer in an ashtray.

Shut up. Shut up. Shut up.
Chanted like a benediction
For a thousandth labored time.
It happened months ago, no one cares
But you when you're drunk.
Katie and Verlin sleep,
And Cory's all but gone,
What's his name's counting the groceries.
Go to bed Annie, go to bed.

I am a painter. Trapped, fighting for life
In a sea of paint. It rises in turpentine swells,
I tip-toe knowing I'll gag if it reaches my mouth.
The crapper don't flush, use the sink.

Tazzie threw it in the tub and ran to his room.
Little bugger. I never give it no thought.

I am here to record. I must record.
Mark down. Make lists. Total up.
Katie One-eye's frying pan face
Looks at me from the floor,
A stream of scarlet birds
From the curling wallpaper
Fly in a V through my eyes
Until my head is full

And something must spill
On to the ancient white sideboard
Where I rest my head. . .
Mustard, jam, vinegar, honey,
Pepper and salt, flour and tea,
Coffee and me looking back
From the bacon grease toaster,
White beer bottles march
A waxen cockroach walk,
Labels squirming
Like Tazzie's rat
In the hangover morning.

THE CLOVE SMUGGLERS

WPK

MOMBASA,Kenya (AP) - Authorities on the Tanzanian
island of Zanzibar have been arresting people for
smuggling cloves into Kenya. Zanzibar is the world's
largest producer of cloves. The penalty for smuggling
cloves is death.

A corps of plotters
curs chasing wealth's mechanical rabbit
bandy the logistics of contraband
about a tin-lined hut:
thieves, panderers, hash-eyed Arabs,
a mercenary smoking a Marlboro,
ferret-faced gun runners, rum traders, and
the inevitable harlot, wiggling her wares,
as she perfumes away the smell of blue steel.

Twenty-two miles away in Mombasa, palates drip,
wadded hands extend toward a hidden cove,
while sauces drip down the globe,
bland as a becalmed sea.

Knuckles of rain rap on corrugated roofs,
a black sailed barque bobs on a moonless bay,
sacks are loaded in thud-filled silence
by men white of eye and white of tooth.

On the Kenyan side, spear-eyed irregulars
lurk like fireflies in jungle fern:
a steamy host waiting to pounce
as a prow grinds sand.

In the flamingo dawn
ghostly puffs from dew-damp guns
send night birds up from the jungle
with a jingling screech
like a shower of silver coin.

Above, the skeletal hands of epicurean chefs,
hover, open, empty, tips dripping blood.

POSES

AK

caught between the glowing tines
of heaven's pitchfork, I squint up into
a farewell sun secure in the love
of the photographer (my father)
who shifts his gaze from background
to foreground (again and again) asking me
to move left or right, as he
composes this one picture: ann,
in the Almighty's embrace, casting
her shadow parallel with the road

>   in time, she'll converse with angels

>   taste the rainbow's indelible signature

>   as it turns to words in her mouth

ann's lover's story is down in black and white -
a script of birthday photos taken when company   came
the family didn't move to town 'til bill was ten,
then he condemned all who longed for farms again
"What's there to miss - chores, chickens, mosquitoes,
mangers, cows and pigs, or spring planting?" the cat,
they'd brought with them; the homemade
furniture, abandoned; hippies carried it away
in the sixties before we could show the girls
the pantry drawers grandma built herself

>   in time, he'll rejoin the angels

>   and be surprised as hell

>   the final chapter hasn't been penned

LOVERS

AK

trapped in the memory of a glacier
we were covered by frozen sky
ground into earth
that had forgotten her sun

encircled by chilling words
written on the limbs
of dismembered trees, when
burning red, tomorrow withdrew

we were rolled into reality, a single
smooth stone totem of winter
below the thaw, yes
we will be found intact.

AND IN A FAR CORNER OF THE WAREHOUSE...

Casey at the Bat - 1988
(or, On First Looking Into Casey's Homer) WPK

On a ballfield green with a velvet sheen
The Mudville nine prepared to play.
What finer sight for the fan's delight
Than Casey batting clean-up on Mudville opening day?

When Mudville came to bat-away
The first three runners filled the bases.
As Casey lumbered t'ward the plate
Expectant smiles lit 10,000 faces.

While Casey swung on the on-deck side,
Glancing ferociously all around,
A stranger walked onto the field,
And stood on the pitching mound.

"I've not been paid for the landscape work,"
He said. "And I'll tell you where it's at,
I want fifteen hundred dollars
Or Casey will never come to bat."

Now Flynn came up with seven,
And Blake did pony four,
Casey himself threw in a dollar,
The manager scrounged up forty more.

The fans gave it their finest effort,
But when the loot was counted up,
They were still a thousand dollars short
Of the sound of, "Batter Up!"

"I reckon the outfield's paid for,"
The stranger said. "As well as second and first.
But I'm laying claim to the pitching mound,
And I'll stay here 'til I burst."

75

The stranger sneered and twirled his mustache
As he taunted the eager crowd,
Until Casey ambled toward the plate,
His manner confident and proud.

What a mighty confrontation!
At the plate Casey pawed the ground:
The landscaper pushed the pitcher aside,
And stalked about the mound.

Ten thousand fans cheered Casey,
And screamed for the stranger's blood.
But Casey smiled and raised a hand
Which stemmed that awful flood.

With one sure stroke Casey saved the day,
A gesture most profound:
For whipping out his MasterCard
Mighty Casey charged the mound.

BIOGRAPHICAL NOTES

Bill (W. P.) Kinsella was born in Alberta in 1935. He spent the first ten years of his life on a farm near Darwell, before moving to Edmonton at age ten. Bill's father, John Matthew, was an American who came to Canada with his parents when he was four, but who never took out Canadian citizenship. John was a building contractor who chose to ranch and feed cattle rather than take welfare during hard times. He served with the U.S. Army Medical Corps in France during the First World War and traveled in the States after the war playing some semipro baseball (third base) before returning to Alberta to marry Olive Elliott in 1928. Bill is an only child. This is his seventeenth book, his first poetry title.

Ann Knight was born in Idaho, in 1943. She lived in six towns in Idaho, Washington, Wyoming, and Montana before she was ten. Her fraternal grandfather emigrated from Sudbury, Ontario, Canada, to the U.S. in the 1870's. Both Ann's parents attended theological seminary during the Depression and served in Baptist churches before meeting and marrying in 1941. Ann is an only child. This is her third book, her first poetry title.

Ann and Bill met in a writing class at the University of Iowa in 1976, and were married in 1978. In Calgary, Alberta, they founded the Calgary Creative Reading Series where they appeared frequently on the open stage to read from work-in-progress. Since retiring to White Rock, B.C., in 1983, to write fulltime, Bill makes about fifty public appearances a year to read from his award-winning fiction, and Ann serves as his part-time secretary/chauffeur/archivist. She is also an active member of the Anglican Parish of St. Mark, Ocean Park.